is an international, independent publishing house and literary journal dedicated to the celebration of music in all its forms. Half Mystic Press publishes carefully crafted books of prose, poetry, and experimental work—invocations of love and wildness, the heartbeat of humanity set to a 4/4 time signature, expanding and redefining unsung narratives, sharp and lamenting, eyes on the horizon. For more information, similar books, and submission guidelines, please visit us at www.halfmystic.com.

"*At the Mercy of the Flies* is a fever that refuses to break. These poems slice through an ever-defamiliarizing world. Each taut stanza grounds the book in the real but twists the birds and sandbags and dandruff into the mystic and ontologically porous, both apocalyptic and transcendent. The surrealism is often eerie and estranging, but just as often personal and intimate. It merges the impossible possibilities to which we've acquiesced with impossible impossibilities that might just liberate us. Matt McBride's poetry is unnerving and alert, joyfully illuminating our current alienations."

Mathias Svalina, author of *Comedy*
and creator of the Dream Delivery Service

At the Mercy of the Flies

Matt McBride

A Half Mystic Press
Publication

FIRST PRINTING, APRIL 2026
HALF MYSTIC PRESS
www.halfmystic.com

© 2026 *by* Matt McBride

Edited *by* Courtney Felle
Assistant edited *by* Lee Anderson
and Kyla-Yến Huỳnh Giffin
Copyedited *by* Ana Mourant

Cover art *by* Sacsthetic
Designed *by* Topaz Winters

ISBN-13: 978-1-948552-20-2
ISBN-10: 1-948552-20-5

For Jess and Selah

Table of Contents

The Mourners Forgot Which Funeral They Were At

Sandbags pillowed
in front of my door
set against a flood of milk.

Bulbs slid loose
from their fixtures.

The night sky
crowned with astronauts

and underneath, me,
covering my hairlessness
with false eyelashes.

In the dream,
I interrupted the autopsies
of every woman I'd slept with,

one after another.
Each day
was its own hospital.

I bruised white
as a peony.

Bathing caps loosened
and everyone's painted clothing went runny.

People dragged other people by their arms
like giant sacks.

Through periods of sleep and unsleep
I cottoned,

suffering a hunger
that fed on its own hungriness.

The bodies kept selling me
on a better disease.

I didn't recognize
my memories anymore.

In paper rooms,
my hands porcelained

as the children
painted their teeth new colors.

There were more collective nouns
than nouns.

There was the time I spent
not learning piano.

A business of flies in my skull recited
commercials for someone else's life.

The bodies repeated themselves
like a cancer.

I wished I was in each passing plane.

I let the children sew
buttons onto my skin.

A point after which
I'd ceased to be promising.

My eyes shelled
like eggs.

I may have been speaking.
It's hard to remember.

Fruit bled when peeled.

The fish kept dying
in the milk.

Everything persisted
at the mercy of the flies

in their beautiful, transparent capes.

Stories of scaffolding
skeletoned no buildings.

I was walking
across the face of a statue
I'd never see.

Each event
a first repetition:

her throat, an extra letter.

Mannequins bobbled
on the painted river.

Buses were comically small
and arms flailed like wind socks
out the windows.

I tied plastic bags
over the children's heads
so they could play astronaut.

Every time I got home,
all my objects
had been wrapped
in Bubble Wrap.

Anything I spoke
was extra.

My reflection blurred
the closer I got to it.

My bedsheets turned
back into smoke.

The rain continued its exegesis
on meaninglessness.

Tape yellowed
and became visible.

Shame waved
like migrations of dead birds

inside me. TVs
all played yesterday.

The bones of small plants.

There were only two people,
and I wasn't one of them.

My mind was a hotel, everyone
locked in their own room.

I detached my hands
before prayer.

The bodies kept asking me
to step into their enormous overcoats.

The light left a chalk behind itself.

Hydrants flooded the streets with milk.

We slept in the fingers
of night's enormous glove.

Our searches resulted in no images.

Passengers drew straws
to see who would land the plane.

Swaddled babies floated like soft pills
two feet off the ground.

I couldn't find a piano,
so I faked it.

The bodies appeared
faceless.

Underneath poorly-drawn trees,
the mourners forgot
which funeral they were at.

My fingers took ovals of color
off of everything I touched.

My shadow made a swishing sound.
I named it *piano*.

One night,
somebody knifed up
the awnings.

I missed the woman
who used to be my wife.

The bodies all put on
their tiny rubber gloves.

Echoes louder than what they echoed.

I had a job
painting over
street signs in white.

I was drowning
in my own little ocean.

In the dream,
I was in a rowboat,

pulling my own dead bodies
out of the water.

A feeling of skinlessness,
an aspirin-like taste.

The missionaries' Bibles
were all blank.

The clouds could've destroyed us.

Printer-paper sky.

Objects carapaced in glue.

I took my turn
washing the last dove,

and when it got dark,
albino rats blanketed me
like a coma.

In the dream,
I was on the set of a sitcom,
crawling behind furniture
to avoid the camera.

Extension cords
wrote drunk signatures
over the surface of the lake.

In the street, the children,
eyes red from a chlorine fog,
waved mannequin limbs like flags.

Yesterday kept taking longer.

Tangles of phone chargers
bushed on sidewalks.

Clouds spoke to each other
with dolls' voices.

I'd run out of feelings
for my words to hold.

Puddled milk curdled
in the street.

All flags came up white.

The children used prescription bottles
as rattles.

Like any fruit left out too long,
my heart began to spoil.

White hair rained.
The dried wings of moths rained.
Torn-up newspapers rained.
Dust, very slowly, rained.
Mineral oil rained.
Expired wedding invitations
rained. The inability to tell guilt from memory
rained. Milk rained. Pearls rained.
Maggots rained. Vodka rained.
Fingernails rained. Wondering if
the fall would kill me rained.
Playing cards with no suits or numbers
rained. Easter grass rained.
Broken porcelain cups rained.
Once, adorably, cotton balls
rained. Piano keys rained.
Fish eyes rained. Fortune cookie fortunes
rained. Laundry powder rained.
Surgical gloves rained. Cigarettes rained.
Seeming and a lack of seeming
rained.

I walked through fields of silver trash,
my skeleton hands
in my pockets.

Graying yarn
trailed from clouds.

Alarms spilled from
one car to the next.

A solid day drink
could get me about 10 percent happier.

Eventually you exhaust
a certain type of courage.

I practiced things to say to her
in hotel rooms.

The light bulbs
filled with milk.

I slept, listening
for the birdstuff
in children's laughter.

I was dying beyond my means.

I called the me *me*,
but I called the nothingness
me too.

The bodies' voices
chandeliered around me.

I scratched off my skin
to get at the tinfoil beneath.

I tried not to see
what I saw in sleep.

I remained faithful to faithlessness.

Mannequins pendulated
from streetlights
with lonely dignity.

I watched myself through the windows
of the dollhouse.

My seat was not a flotation device.

I was a hole
the world fell through.

In the dream,
a man threw dolls
down the well.

Office carpeting
covered the ground.

The planes landed
without any people in them.

I waded through crowds of children
with their hands raised,

tugging on their arms
to make sure they believed.

I imagined her carrying a dead dog
like a handbag.

I imagined my soul
as a bottle of gnats.

I spent my nights at the café
drinking a warm glass of chalk.

The Age Of

Jesus came back,
and we pinned him
to a great sheet of Styrofoam
like a dried butterfly.

This all happened
during the waning years
of the Grass Age.

There was a seriousness of periods.

We moved so it looked like
our shadows were drinking
from each other.

We sought
workable flex schedules.

We reported the sea
lost at sea.

Our coffins
were the only boats
we needed.

Inside the Dollar General,
my head was a balloon
made of metalated plastic,

my face a slogan among slogans,
plain as unbranded glue.

I ate Peeps
from a dishwashing glove.

I imagined a beautiful horse
choking on me
when I died.

Every day, I left
a mannequin of myself behind.

I glued pennies to my skin
like a disease.

Teeth mushroomed on tree trunks.
Empty body bags lay everywhere.

Seven children played at
keeping an inflated surgical glove aloft.

Two years later,
the War of No Touching would start.

Our thoughts covered everything in dandruff.
Trees sagged with taxidermied birds.

The sea so full of messages in bottles
it sounded like a xylophone—

and night, a great clower of pupils,
made a vast darkness without us.

The Age of Broken Bottles on the Sidewalk
took its last, ragged breaths.

We stayed apologetically ourselves.

I wore dishwashing gloves
for everything but washing dishes.

I made Etch A Sketch self-portraits
no one wanted to buy.

A string of ants trailed behind me
like an unplugged power cord,

heralding that the Age of Meaningless Omens
had begun in earnest.

I wondered where everyone
got those air horns
I kept hearing.

My daughter held real celebrity
at area nursing facilities.

Statistically speaking,
I was halfway dead.

Clouds cooed like doves
as bruises doilied under our skin.

It was sometime
during the Age of Everyone's It.

We'd scatter like pink roaches,
then stand still
as crucifixes without a cross.

The grass was waves of fingers
pointing at nothing.

Every sign depicted a hand
making a gun shape.

I imagined what I looked like
in the Dollar General's surveillance footage.

There was a G.I. Joe
of every bully from my high school

and a blanket printed
with a mountain I'd never see.

My heart was a parking lot
with many open spaces.

The air smelled
like a well-remodeled basement.

Every garage door in Ohio opened,
and all the UPS drivers

looked ready to strip
for a bachelorette party.

Late May, perhaps.

My daughter chased taxidermied rabbits
in the grass lot next door.

The municipal worker in her neon vest
sold tickets to use the excavator.

In my notebook,
I wrote *birds*
with a question mark,

but it wasn't a question.

A Starbucks cup practiced its vowels
as it rolled over the asphalt.

One man threw
a cigarette on the sidewalk

and one following pinched it up
for a last inhale.

The migration and mitigation of things.

A child's bike,
spokes covered with tinfoil
to look like chrome rims.

I couldn't tell which part
was supposed to be the revolution,
so I pretended to be more people.

I decided to stop seeing my savior.

I titled a poem
Poem with a Hole in the Middle,

and posted it to my list
of things that happened while I was still alive.

A thousand redheaded undergraduates,
each carrying a plastic grocery bag,
paraded by my window

as I inflated a ream of doves.

What I mean to say
is that the bell of myself was still,
that my heart felt taxidermied.

A solitary plane
crossed a solitary sky.

In the end, the war was just another
multilevel marketing scheme.

The fluorescents reached quorum
at the Dollar General
outside Moscow, Tennessee.

There was an asbestos tile
for each day of my life.

Triplets in sweatpants
formed a line behind
the unmanned register.

It felt like a crime scene
waiting for a crime.

We lived high in the voices,
a sum of ordinary vices.

The dead weren't waiting for us,
though we wanted to think so.

Stars lingered, mines left over
from a war no one remembered.

What was truth to us?

A special kind of nothing
we built every box for.

So many wrong things
weren't wrong things.

I want to say we didn't
make our choices willingly,

want to say
we didn't pucker up and blow

when the Lord of Flies
whistled a new anthem

as he returned triumphant
from Hell.

Our shadows were spills of mirror.

Our hearts, paper lanterns
crowding an overproduced sky.

We lived in the moment
after the moment after orgasm.

Some things
we weren't greater than.

We wrapped every tree
in aluminum foil

as night held
its silent auction

of the same dead stars.

Birds got stuck
in the cellophane sky.

Behind the sky,
the never-ending chime
of an open car door.

We carried gravel in cupped hands,
made ourselves crowns of chicory.

We spent our lives
walking along the black river.

We left a trail of Christmas lights
to find our way back
to nowhere.

The Party

Spent extinguishers
left a perpetual fog.

Cement trucks of margarita mix.
Sunsets iridescent as gasoline's skin.

We took every stone
from the cemetery.

We were like the plastic food
inside a vitrine. We were

some of the only people alive.

All animals had transparent skin.
Finger bushes touched us

as we walked past. Each moment
opened to nothing.

Shadows assumed
a graphic function.

Leftover confetti
scabbed to paper-mache.

On Saturn's table we lay
naked, powdered with sugar.

We elected whoever
wore the worst wig president,

painted faces on watermelons
for the inauguration.

To hide our smallnesses,
we built bigger homes. Each day

was a new lifestyle vlog.
The soft meaninglessness

of clouds
stuffed the unstuffed space.

And when we ran out of confetti,
we used broken glass.

On inflatable furniture,
we waded a cultural pause.

Strands of hair
thickened the wind.

Fifty thousand flies
erected the carnival in a day.

Drunk ballerinas
played Twister onstage.

When surveyed, we replied
We are good.

I had a good job
at the velvet supply company.

I drove my own empty bus.

Feelings extended like highways
away from me.

On every bill,
our president winked.

The pervasive smell of
the inside of a microwave.

I belonged
to the siren's congregation.

I lived my life
as if invited.

Between the first and last letter
of usernames,

the website put asterisks,
making everyone a unique obscenity.

Our dreams frayed at the edges
as we moved closer to light sources.

The music was always Donna Summer,
the way she could make love last four syllables.

What isn't better scaled in sequins?
We pushed the tempo faster than we could sing.

This world could never be
big enough for itself.

The stars dripped
paint primer. Everywhere
white eyelets mushroomed.

Our shadows lay folded
outside Rubbermaid urns.

When our president took the stage,
we tore pages out of books
in applause.

We pretended
the haired mold was grass.

Of all the emotions,
why not choose awe?

Our messiahs were the families
who came with the picture frame.

Many-hearted, we felt
like the skin of a dove
before feathers appear.

Nickel-plated sky.
Trucks shrouded in bedsheets.

Hotels holding
a gun in each nightstand.

Crocheted trees
connected like paper dolls.

We communicated solely by postcards
attached to balloons.

On beige carpets we coted like doves,
ate cheese off of wooden boards.

Our crepe paper flowers
ruined with every rain.

At dusk, police in white suits
choked to death the people left

outside. Pigeons concreted
in their voices' wake.

Candied-glass windows
muddled sound enough

that we could tell ourselves
they weren't screaming

I can't breathe,
but rather, *I believe,*

and we repeated it
as a prayer to bring sleep.

My days pigeon-stitched,
gratuitous with clouds.

Nights were spent
eating leftover sheet cakes,

their occasions forgotten.
The iced letters bled

admonishments of the leaf blowers
I used to sweep popped balloons off of lawns.

My imagination was a ranch house
with porcelain horses on each end table.

In the basement,
my heart:

a Midwestern kid at a drum kit,
starting into the most boring solo.

Every hat was disposable.

Conversation was one long game
of two truths and a lie.

All four oceans drained
to make great ball pits.

When our president
promised us nothing,

we took all of it.

Everyone was familiar
as passengers on the same flight.

Our Mad Libs newspapers
had dotted rectangles,

so we could glue on
whatever pictures we wanted.

Love didn't redeem; it just
let us forget ourselves. Sometimes,

overnight, a rain of pearls
clogged the roads.

The parade looped:

coffins strewn on a flatbed
like a Jenga loss;

other people's children, costumeless,
playing instruments
they hadn't learned to play.

Onlookers reapplied their lipstick.

No sentiments
that couldn't be spray-painted
onto a bedsheet.

Another flatbed carried
everything I'd ever owned,
still in the original packaging.

I felt an overwhelming desire
to pet the service animals.

The piñata was filled
with titles for used cars.

Everyone's phone rang
simultaneously.

No sleeve was without tassels.

We wriggled like
gummy worms in candy compost.

There were meat raffles;
there were weird ponies.

Though blindfolded,
we could see a little
but didn't want to ruin the game.

Knowing half of the lyrics
was justification enough

to join the song.

Our president sounded tinny
from inside the phone:

We live in imaginary times.
He was a man statued before doves.

There are too many names.
His voice sounded like traffic.

We were trapped, all,
inside the heart's meat closet.

Pick any name you want
as long as it rhymes with mine.

There were many things we could believe,
and this was one of them.

I was listed in the credits as *body*.

My white noise machine
played sounds of crystal
breaking.

I wore children's clothes.

The bird of my heart
flew into every window.

I owned a coffee table book
of Big Mac photographs.

The flag on my car showed
I wanted to be part of
the same funeral
as everyone else.

We used Instagram to make sure
our dreams were consistent.

It was all one big beast fable
with no moral, though

morale was high. We divined
from ramen noodles' cursive.

We couldn't remember which yesterday
we missed so much.

Nightly, we stormed the landfills
and dug up our lost toys.

Doves in their tiny capes
flew above our president as he spoke:

*I dream that behind this wall
there are a thousand walls.*

We admired
the TV's resolution.

Our arm hairs grew thicker
with every word:

*These days are
an ever-expanding warehouse.*

This thought,
made of the same words
as any other,

could also have been true.

We grew like goldfish,
big as our glass walls allowed.

We were plastic dolls
watching elephants.

Our intestines coiled
tight as a baseball's yarn.

Rain made the city
a dance floor.

Time sidled like
pictures in a View-Master,

scenes recycling until
we tired of pulling the lever

and focused instead on finding new citrus
for infusion into IPAs

whose names were puns
on the names of '90s sitcom characters.

All that and less.

Some days, we'd go to Aldi's
and undress.

We were, everyone, extras
in an endless post-credits scene.

Glitter sternutated
from the bell of the sky.

Console televisions played
our president's third inaugural address:

When I went to Europe
and saw the Old Masters,

I was involved
with the credibility of the drama.

Would Christ on the cross,
if he opened his eyes,

believe the spectators?

Papal white overcast.

My pregnant wife duned
under the sheets.

I spent my mornings transcribing
the sky's unwritten letters.

Candles big as telephone poles
replaced the trees.

I kept forgetting to subject.

We used asbestos as snow
so the cotton batting wouldn't catch.

Everything
was covered in my skin,

and I was startled
by how much life was in my life.

Someone spray-painted *Ho Ho Ho*
on the inside of their windows

so the outside read *oH oH oH,*
still in orgasm seasons later.

A karaoke machine harnessed
to a boy riding a bicycle,
his soundtrack sewing the day to itself.

The tail lights of a delivery truck blinked
in Morse code, announcing no emergency.

Three plastic sheep
on a windowsill in the laundromat.

Anything more than one person singing
counted as a chorus.

The city's steeples
like half-empty glue bottles.

Acid wash sky.

There was just enough
to beg for.

Police let the children take turns
holding their guns.

Nooses made of Christmas lights
swayed from the trees.

We tore every curtain to ribbons
so there'd be enough blindfolds.

Bleach-boned mannequins
wore T-shirts celebrating
Black History Month at Target.

Ambulances played Katy Perry
to avoid startling.

Some of us wanted the same,
and some of us wanted the same
called something different.

The plastic cutlery
wouldn't tear the napkin skin of our wrists.

All pills were replaced with Skittles.

Our president won his fifth election
on a memory correction platform.

Empty Pepsi cups fell
from stadia of cloud.

Communal games
lent us purpose.

A low horizon line
obscured the vanishing points.

Each looked to the other when asked,
Who dropped the heart's teacup?

People tied mannequins
to car roofs like deer.

I had a job
sewing eggs together.

I collected stars
in a teacup for Selah.

The wind was a brush
of drunken voices.

In sleep, I walked naked
through a forest of arms.

Plastic plants
grew more convincing.

A tea set
made from human skin.

A great nothing
happening.

During the long fall of sleep,
we saw escalators
descend into an ocean.

Ambiguity
about when we should leave.

Store alarms in mini-malls
rose and fell with the sun.

The city started its perpetual yard sale.
Everyone, without invitation, looking

like leftover Guess Who? characters.
In the wake of the wake of, life

progressed like a book of carpet samples.
Every refrigerator's hum
dropped an octave, chanting:

This is the way the world ends
This is the way the world ends
This is the way the world ends—

it doesn't.

Notes

"Our shadows were spills of mirror ...": This poem is inspired by Yeah Yeah Yeahs's song "Spitting Off the Edge of the World."

"All animals had transparent skin ...": The line "shadows assume a graphic function" is from Sheldon Nodelman's book *The Rothko Chapel Paintings: Origins, Structure, Meaning.*

"We were, everyone, extras ...": The italicized lines are from a 1958 lecture given by Mark Rothko at the Pratt Institute.

"The city started its perpetual yard sale ...": The italicized lines are from T. S. Eliot's poem "The Hollow Men."

Acknowledgements

First, I want to thank the staff of Half Mystic. Thank you to Topaz Winters for seeing the potential here. Thank you to Courtney Felle, Kyla-Yến Huỳnh Giffin, and Lee Anderson for your thoughtful edits, which made this the book it is. *At the Mercy of the Flies* would not exist without your vision, skill, and sacrifice.

I want to thank the editors of the following journals where these poems first appeared, sometimes under different titles:

Across the Margin: "I practiced things to say to her ...," "I walked through fields of silver trash ...," "My fingers took ovals of color ...," "Swaddled babies floated like soft pills ...," "Hydrants flooded the streets with milk ..."

Action, Spectacle: "Clouds cooed like doves ...," "Every day, I left ...," "Our thoughts covered everything in dandruff ...," "Every hat was disposable ...," "Our messiahs were ...," "We elected whoever ..."

After the Pause: "Bathing caps loosened ...," "The bodies all put on ...," "Fruit bled when peeled ...," "In the dream, / I was in a rowboat ...," "Printer paper sky ..."

Banyan Review: "Spent extinguishers ...," "The piñata was filled ...," "We grew like goldfish ..."

The Collidescope: "Jesus came back ..."

Figure 1: "On inflatable furniture ...," "People tied mannequins ...," "We used Instagram ..."

Map Literary: "Sandbags pillowed ...," "In the dream, / I interrupted the autopsies ...," "Every time I got home ...," "Mannequins bobbled ...," "Tape yellowed ...," "There were more collective nouns ..."

Packingtown Review: "Puddled milk curdled ...," "I let the children ...," "Mannequins pendulumed ...," "My mind was a hotel ...," "Yesterday kept taking longer ..."

Puerto del Sol: "In the Dollar General ..."

Rejection Letters: "Every garage door in Ohio opened ..."

The Rupture: "Our days pigeon-stitched ...," "Between the first and last letter ..."

Rust + Moth: "The parade looped ..."

A particularly big thank you to Carl Annarummo of Greying Ghost, who published "The Mourners Forgot Which Funeral They Were At" as a limited-edition chapbook.

Thank you to my writing group: Ellen Elder, Eric Bliman, Heather Hamilton, and Michelle Burke.

Thank you to the friends who supported me and my poetry while writing this book: Byron Kanoti, Brian Trapp, Leah McCormack and Dietrick Vanderhill, Jim Condron, Linwood Rumney, Manuel Iris, Mark Jenkins, and Seth Fried.

Thank you to Wilson College for your faith in me and my work, and to my colleagues at the college for your friendship.

Thank you to Philip Lindsey for letting me into your studio.

Thank you to Melissa Helton for asking me to be a mentor at the Ironwood Writers Studio, and for welcoming me to the Hindman School.

Thank you to Noah Falck, fellow lost son of Dayton and my brother in the craft.

Thank you to Tessa Mellas. You have always been my most honest reader and most unwavering advocate.

Thank you to C. A. Diltz and Richard McBride for teaching me that art matters.

And thank you to all others whose support has been essential. Please know that while your name might not be written here, it is written somewhere on the walls of my heart.

Finally, thank you to Jess and Selah. I thought the party was over until you two came into my life.

About the Author

Matt McBride is the author of two full-length collections, *City of Incandescent Light* (Black Lawrence, 2018) and *At the Mercy of the Flies* (Half Mystic, 2026), as well as four chapbooks. His most recent, *Prerecorded Weather*, co-written with Noah Falck, is available from Survision Books. He is the winner of the James Tate Prize, the St. Lawrence Book Award, and the Ohio Chapbook Award. He is the recipient of an Ohio Arts Council grant, an Elliston Poetry Fellowship, and a Writers in the Heartland residency. Currently, he lives in Chambersburg, PA, where he teaches composition, literature, and creative writing at Wilson College. Find him online at www.mattmcbridepoetry.com.